# EFFICIENCY IN YOUR POCKET

## YOUR MONTHLY PLANNER MADE SMALL

Flash Planners and Notebooks

*Flash Planners and Notebooks*

JOURNALS & NOTEBOOKS

# THIS BOOK BELONGS TO

_____

# ☞ MONTHLY PLANNER

| Mon | Tue | Wed | Thurs | Fri | Sat | Sun |
|-----|-----|-----|-------|-----|-----|-----|
|     |     |     |       |     |     |     |
|     |     |     |       |     |     |     |
|     |     |     |       |     |     |     |
|     |     |     |       |     |     |     |
|     |     |     |       |     |     |     |
|     |     |     |       |     |     |     |
|     |     |     |       |     |     |     |

# 👉 MONTHLY CHECKLIST

| SHOPPING LIST | KIDS LIST |
|---|---|

★ _____
★ _____
★ _____
★ _____
★ _____
★ _____
★ _____
★ _____
★ _____

★ _____
★ _____
★ _____
★ _____
★ _____
★ _____
★ _____
★ _____
★ _____

| DINNER DATES | PLAY DATES |
|---|---|

👉 # KEEP TRACK

## QUOTE OF THE MONTH

## BILLS TO PAY

| | |
|---|---|
| | |
| | |
| | |
| | |
| | |
| | |
| | |
| | |
| | |
| | |

## I'M GRATEFUL FOR

## NOTES

# WEEKLY MEETING

MONDAY

FRIDAY

TUESDAY

SATURDAY

WEDNESDAY

SUNDAY

THURSDAY

NOTES

# TO DO

❖      ❖      ❖      ❖

❖      ❖      ❖      ❖

❖      ❖      ❖      ❖

❖      ❖      ❖      ❖

❖      ❖      ❖      ❖

❖      ❖      ❖      ❖

❖      ❖      ❖      ❖

❖      ❖      ❖      ❖

❖      ❖      ❖      ❖

# DINNER MEETINGS

| MON | TUE | WED | THURS |
|-----|-----|-----|-------|
|     |     |     |       |

| FRI | SAT | SUN | |
|-----|-----|-----|---|
|     |     |     |   |

# REMINDERS

# ☛ MONTHLY PLANNER

| Mon | Tue | Wed | Thurs | Fri | Sat | Sun |
|-----|-----|-----|-------|-----|-----|-----|
|     |     |     |       |     |     |     |
|     |     |     |       |     |     |     |
|     |     |     |       |     |     |     |
|     |     |     |       |     |     |     |
|     |     |     |       |     |     |     |
|     |     |     |       |     |     |     |
|     |     |     |       |     |     |     |
|     |     |     |       |     |     |     |

# 👉 MONTHLY CHECKLIST

| SHOPPING LIST |
|---|

★ _____

★ _____

★ _____

★ _____

★ _____

★ _____

★ _____

★ _____

★ _____

| KIDS LIST |
|---|

★ _____

★ _____

★ _____

★ _____

★ _____

★ _____

★ _____

★ _____

★ _____

| DINNER DATES |
|---|

| PLAY DATES |
|---|

# 👉 KEEP TRACK

## QUOTE OF THE MONTH

## BILLS TO PAY

|  |  |
|--|--|
|  |  |
|  |  |
|  |  |
|  |  |
|  |  |
|  |  |
|  |  |
|  |  |
|  |  |
|  |  |

## I'M GRATEFUL FOR

## NOTES

# TO DO

✤
✤
✤
✤
✤
✤
✤
✤
✤

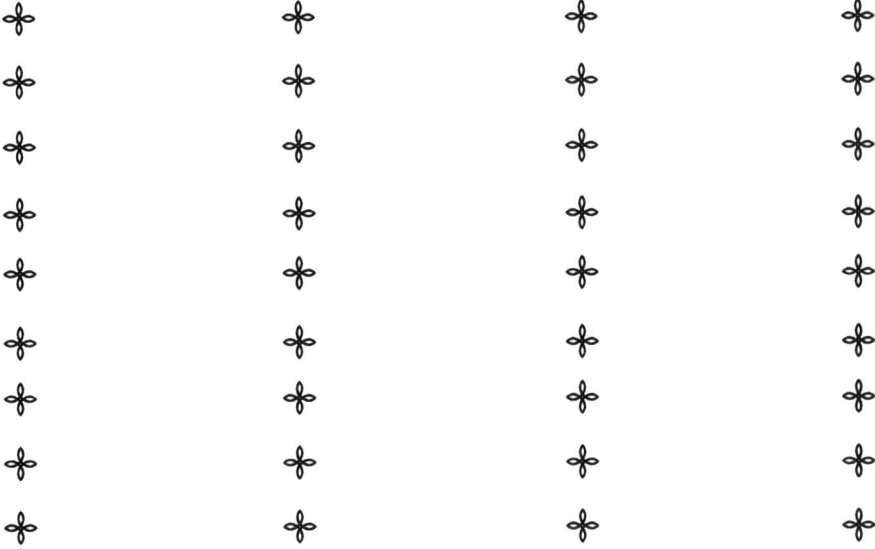

# DINNER MEETINGS

| MON | TUE | WED | THURS |
|---|---|---|---|
| | | | |

| FRI | SAT | SUN | |
|---|---|---|---|
| | | | |

# REMINDERS

# WEEKLY MEETING

MONDAY

FRIDAY

TUESDAY

SATURDAY

WEDNESDAY

SUNDAY

THURSDAY

NOTES

# 👉 MONTHLY PLANNER

| Mon | Tue | Wed | Thurs | Fri | Sat | Sun |
|-----|-----|-----|-------|-----|-----|-----|
|     |     |     |       |     |     |     |
|     |     |     |       |     |     |     |
|     |     |     |       |     |     |     |
|     |     |     |       |     |     |     |
|     |     |     |       |     |     |     |
|     |     |     |       |     |     |     |
|     |     |     |       |     |     |     |

# ☛ MONTHLY CHECKLIST

| SHOPPING LIST | KIDS LIST |
|---|---|

★ _____     ★ _____

★ _____     ★ _____

★ _____     ★ _____

★ _____     ★ _____

★ _____     ★ _____

★ _____     ★ _____

★ _____     ★ _____

★ _____     ★ _____

★ _____     ★ _____

| DINNER DATES | PLAY DATES |
|---|---|

# 👉 KEEP TRACK

## QUOTE OF THE MONTH

## BILLS TO PAY

| | |
|---|---|
| | |
| | |
| | |
| | |
| | |
| | |
| | |
| | |
| | |
| | |

## I'M GRATEFUL FOR

## NOTES

# WEEKLY MEETING

MONDAY

FRIDAY

TUESDAY

SATURDAY

WEDNESDAY

SUNDAY

THURSDAY

NOTES

# TO DO

✦        ✦        ✦        ✦

✦        ✦        ✦        ✦

✦        ✦        ✦        ✦

✦        ✦        ✦        ✦

✦        ✦        ✦        ✦

✦        ✦        ✦        ✦

✦        ✦        ✦        ✦

✦        ✦        ✦        ✦

✦        ✦        ✦        ✦

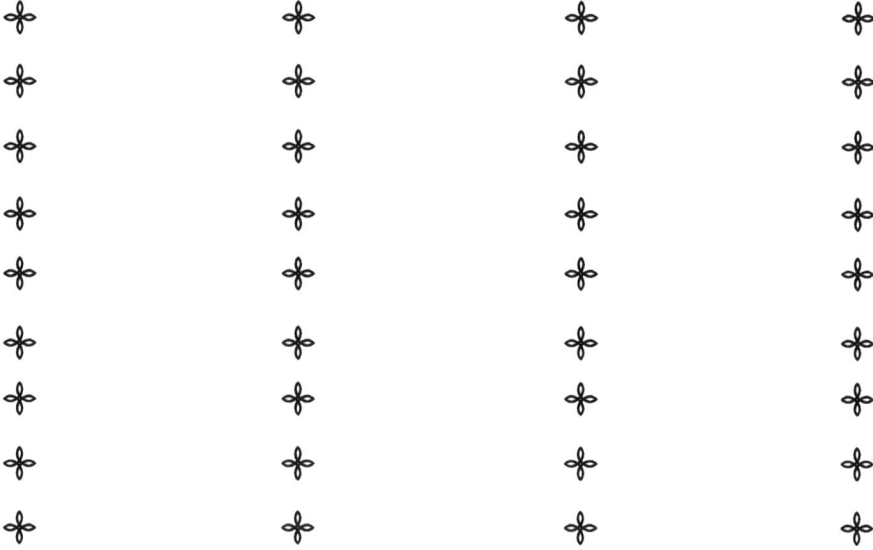

# DINNER MEETINGS

| MON | TUE | WED | THURS |
|---|---|---|---|
|  |  |  |  |
| FRI | SAT | SUN |  |
|  |  |  |  |

# REMINDERS

# MONTHLY PLANNER

| Mon | Tue | Wed | Thurs | Fri | Sat | Sun |
|-----|-----|-----|-------|-----|-----|-----|
|     |     |     |       |     |     |     |
|     |     |     |       |     |     |     |
|     |     |     |       |     |     |     |
|     |     |     |       |     |     |     |
|     |     |     |       |     |     |     |
|     |     |     |       |     |     |     |
|     |     |     |       |     |     |     |

# 👉 MONTHLY CHECKLIST

| SHOPPING LIST | KIDS LIST |
|---|---|

★ _____

★ _____

★ _____

★ _____

★ _____

★ _____

★ _____

★ _____

★ _____

★ _____

★ _____

★ _____

★ _____

★ _____

★ _____

★ _____

★ _____

★ _____

| DINNER DATES | PLAY DATES |
|---|---|

# 👉 KEEP TRACK

## QUOTE OF THE MONTH

## BILLS TO PAY

| | |
|---|---|
| | |
| | |
| | |
| | |
| | |
| | |
| | |
| | |
| | |
| | |
| | |

## I'M GRATEFUL FOR

## NOTES

# TO DO

❖      ❖      ❖      ❖

❖      ❖      ❖      ❖

❖      ❖      ❖      ❖

❖      ❖      ❖      ❖

❖      ❖      ❖      ❖

❖      ❖      ❖      ❖

❖      ❖      ❖      ❖

❖      ❖      ❖      ❖

❖      ❖      ❖      ❖

# DINNER MEETINGS

| MON | TUE | WED | THURS |
|---|---|---|---|
|  |  |  |  |

| FRI | SAT | SUN | |
|---|---|---|---|
|  |  |  |  |

# REMINDERS

# WEEKLY MEETING

| MONDAY | FRIDAY |
|--------|--------|

| TUESDAY | SATURDAY |
|---------|----------|

| WEDNESDAY | SUNDAY |
|-----------|--------|

| THURSDAY | NOTES |
|----------|-------|

# ☛ MONTHLY PLANNER

| Mon | Tue | Wed | Thurs | Fri | Sat | Sun |
|-----|-----|-----|-------|-----|-----|-----|
|     |     |     |       |     |     |     |
|     |     |     |       |     |     |     |
|     |     |     |       |     |     |     |
|     |     |     |       |     |     |     |
|     |     |     |       |     |     |     |
|     |     |     |       |     |     |     |
|     |     |     |       |     |     |     |
|     |     |     |       |     |     |     |

# MONTHLY CHECKLIST

| SHOPPING LIST | KIDS LIST |
|---|---|

★ _____
★ _____
★ _____
★ _____
★ _____
★ _____
★ _____
★ _____
★ _____

★ _____
★ _____
★ _____
★ _____
★ _____
★ _____
★ _____
★ _____
★ _____

| DINNER DATES | PLAY DATES |
|---|---|

# 👉 KEEP TRACK

## QUOTE OF THE MONTH

## BILLS TO PAY

| | |
|---|---|
| | |
| | |
| | |
| | |
| | |
| | |
| | |
| | |
| | |
| | |

## I'M GRATEFUL FOR

## NOTES

# WEEKLY MEETING

MONDAY

FRIDAY

TUESDAY

SATURDAY

WEDNESDAY

SUNDAY

THURSDAY

NOTES

# TO DO

✦      ✦      ✦      ✦

✦      ✦      ✦      ✦

✦      ✦      ✦      ✦

✦      ✦      ✦      ✦

✦      ✦      ✦      ✦

✦      ✦      ✦      ✦

✦      ✦      ✦      ✦

✦      ✦      ✦      ✦

✦      ✦      ✦      ✦

# DINNER MEETINGS

| MON | TUE | WED | THURS |
|---|---|---|---|
| | | | |

| FRI | SAT | SUN | |
|---|---|---|---|
| | | | |

# REMINDERS

# ☛ MONTHLY PLANNER

| Mon | Tue | Wed | Thurs | Fri | Sat | Sun |
|-----|-----|-----|-------|-----|-----|-----|
|     |     |     |       |     |     |     |
|     |     |     |       |     |     |     |
|     |     |     |       |     |     |     |
|     |     |     |       |     |     |     |
|     |     |     |       |     |     |     |
|     |     |     |       |     |     |     |
|     |     |     |       |     |     |     |

# 👉 MONTHLY CHECKLIST

| SHOPPING LIST | KIDS LIST |
|---|---|

★ _____

★ _____

★ _____

★ _____

★ _____

★ _____

★ _____

★ _____

★ _____

★ _____

★ _____

★ _____

★ _____

★ _____

★ _____

★ _____

★ _____

★ _____

| DINNER DATES | PLAY DATES |
|---|---|

# 👉 KEEP TRACK

## QUOTE OF THE MONTH

## BILLS TO PAY

| | |
|---|---|
| | |
| | |
| | |
| | |
| | |
| | |
| | |
| | |
| | |
| | |

## I'M GRATEFUL FOR

## NOTES

# TO DO

❖          ❖          ❖          ❖

❖          ❖          ❖          ❖

❖          ❖          ❖          ❖

❖          ❖          ❖          ❖

❖          ❖          ❖          ❖

❖          ❖          ❖          ❖

❖          ❖          ❖          ❖

❖          ❖          ❖          ❖

❖          ❖          ❖          ❖

## DINNER MEETINGS

| MON | TUE | WED | THURS |
|-----|-----|-----|-------|
|     |     |     |       |

| FRI | SAT | SUN | |
|-----|-----|-----|--|
|     |     |     |  |

## REMINDERS

# WEEKLY MEETING

| MONDAY | FRIDAY |
|--------|--------|

| TUESDAY | SATURDAY |
|---------|----------|

| WEDNESDAY | SUNDAY |
|-----------|--------|

| THURSDAY | NOTES |
|----------|-------|

# ☛ MONTHLY PLANNER

| Mon | Tue | Wed | Thurs | Fri | Sat | Sun |
|-----|-----|-----|-------|-----|-----|-----|
|     |     |     |       |     |     |     |
|     |     |     |       |     |     |     |
|     |     |     |       |     |     |     |
|     |     |     |       |     |     |     |
|     |     |     |       |     |     |     |
|     |     |     |       |     |     |     |
|     |     |     |       |     |     |     |

# ☞ MONTHLY CHECKLIST

| SHOPPING LIST | KIDS LIST |
|---|---|

★ _____
★ _____
★ _____
★ _____
★ _____
★ _____
★ _____
★ _____
★ _____

★ _____
★ _____
★ _____
★ _____
★ _____
★ _____
★ _____
★ _____
★ _____

| DINNER DATES | PLAY DATES |
|---|---|

# 👉 KEEP TRACK

## QUOTE OF THE MONTH

## BILLS TO PAY

## I'M GRATEFUL FOR

## NOTES

# WEEKLY MEETING

MONDAY

FRIDAY

TUESDAY

SATURDAY

WEDNESDAY

SUNDAY

THURSDAY

NOTES

## TO DO

�֎  ✖  ✖  ✖
✖  ✖  ✖  ✖
✖  ✖  ✖  ✖
✖  ✖  ✖  ✖
✖  ✖  ✖  ✖
✖  ✖  ✖  ✖
✖  ✖  ✖  ✖
✖  ✖  ✖  ✖
✖  ✖  ✖  ✖

## DINNER MEETINGS

| MON | TUE | WED | THURS |
|-----|-----|-----|-------|
|     |     |     |       |
| FRI | SAT | SUN |       |
|     |     |     |       |

## REMINDERS

# ☛ MONTHLY PLANNER

| Mon | Tue | Wed | Thurs | Fri | Sat | Sun |
|-----|-----|-----|-------|-----|-----|-----|
|     |     |     |       |     |     |     |
|     |     |     |       |     |     |     |
|     |     |     |       |     |     |     |
|     |     |     |       |     |     |     |
|     |     |     |       |     |     |     |
|     |     |     |       |     |     |     |
|     |     |     |       |     |     |     |
|     |     |     |       |     |     |     |

# MONTHLY CHECKLIST

| SHOPPING LIST |
|---|

★ _____

★ _____

★ _____

★ _____

★ _____

★ _____

★ _____

★ _____

★ _____

| KIDS LIST |
|---|

★ _____

★ _____

★ _____

★ _____

★ _____

★ _____

★ _____

★ _____

★ _____

| DINNER DATES |
|---|

| PLAY DATES |
|---|

# 👉 KEEP TRACK

## QUOTE OF THE MONTH

## BILLS TO PAY

| | |
|---|---|
| | |
| | |
| | |
| | |
| | |
| | |
| | |
| | |
| | |
| | |

## I'M GRATEFUL FOR

## NOTES

# WEEKLY MEETING

MONDAY

FRIDAY

TUESDAY

SATURDAY

WEDNESDAY

SUNDAY

THURSDAY

NOTES

# TO DO

❖      ❖      ❖      ❖

❖      ❖      ❖      ❖

❖      ❖      ❖      ❖

❖      ❖      ❖      ❖

❖      ❖      ❖      ❖

❖      ❖      ❖      ❖

❖      ❖      ❖      ❖

❖      ❖      ❖      ❖

❖      ❖      ❖      ❖

# DINNER MEETINGS

| MON | TUE | WED | THURS |
| --- | --- | --- | --- |
| | | | |

| FRI | SAT | SUN | |
| --- | --- | --- | --- |
| | | | |

# REMINDERS

# ☛ MONTHLY PLANNER

| Mon | Tue | Wed | Thurs | Fri | Sat | Sun |
|-----|-----|-----|-------|-----|-----|-----|
|     |     |     |       |     |     |     |
|     |     |     |       |     |     |     |
|     |     |     |       |     |     |     |
|     |     |     |       |     |     |     |
|     |     |     |       |     |     |     |
|     |     |     |       |     |     |     |
|     |     |     |       |     |     |     |

# MONTHLY CHECKLIST

| SHOPPING LIST |
|---|

★ _____

★ _____

★ _____

★ _____

★ _____

★ _____

★ _____

★ _____

★ _____

| KIDS LIST |
|---|

★ _____

★ _____

★ _____

★ _____

★ _____

★ _____

★ _____

★ _____

★ _____

| DINNER DATES |
|---|

| PLAY DATES |
|---|

# ☛ KEEP TRACK

## QUOTE OF THE MONTH

## BILLS TO PAY

## I'M GRATEFUL FOR

## NOTES

# TO DO

✦       ✦       ✦       ✦

✦       ✦       ✦       ✦

✦       ✦       ✦       ✦

✦       ✦       ✦       ✦

✦       ✦       ✦       ✦

✦       ✦       ✦       ✦

✦       ✦       ✦       ✦

✦       ✦       ✦       ✦

✦       ✦       ✦       ✦

# DINNER MEETINGS

| MON | TUE | WED | THURS |
|---|---|---|---|
| | | | |

| FRI | SAT | SUN | |
|---|---|---|---|
| | | | |

# REMINDERS

# WEEKLY MEETING

MONDAY

FRIDAY

TUESDAY

SATURDAY

WEDNESDAY

SUNDAY

THURSDAY

NOTES

# ☛ MONTHLY PLANNER

| Mon | Tue | Wed | Thurs | Fri | Sat | Sun |
|-----|-----|-----|-------|-----|-----|-----|
|     |     |     |       |     |     |     |
|     |     |     |       |     |     |     |
|     |     |     |       |     |     |     |
|     |     |     |       |     |     |     |
|     |     |     |       |     |     |     |
|     |     |     |       |     |     |     |
|     |     |     |       |     |     |     |

# MONTHLY CHECKLIST

| SHOPPING LIST | KIDS LIST |
|---|---|

★ _____     ★ _____

★ _____     ★ _____

★ _____     ★ _____

★ _____     ★ _____

★ _____     ★ _____

★ _____     ★ _____

★ _____     ★ _____

★ _____     ★ _____

★ _____     ★ _____

| DINNER DATES | PLAY DATES |
|---|---|

# 👉 KEEP TRACK

## QUOTE OF THE MONTH

## BILLS TO PAY

| | |
|---|---|
| | |
| | |
| | |
| | |
| | |
| | |
| | |
| | |
| | |
| | |

## I'M GRATEFUL FOR

## NOTES

# WEEKLY MEETING

MONDAY

FRIDAY

TUESDAY

SATURDAY

WEDNESDAY

SUNDAY

THURSDAY

NOTES

# TO DO

| | | | |
|---|---|---|---|
| ✥ | ✥ | ✥ | ✥ |
| ✥ | ✥ | ✥ | ✥ |
| ✥ | ✥ | ✥ | ✥ |
| ✥ | ✥ | ✥ | ✥ |
| ✥ | ✥ | ✥ | ✥ |
| ✥ | ✥ | ✥ | ✥ |
| ✥ | ✥ | ✥ | ✥ |
| ✥ | ✥ | ✥ | ✥ |
| ✥ | ✥ | ✥ | ✥ |

## DINNER MEETINGS

| MON | TUE | WED | THURS |
|---|---|---|---|
| | | | |

| FRI | SAT | SUN | |
|---|---|---|---|
| | | | |

## REMINDERS

# ☛ MONTHLY PLANNER

| Mon | Tue | Wed | Thurs | Fri | Sat | Sun |
|-----|-----|-----|-------|-----|-----|-----|
|     |     |     |       |     |     |     |
|     |     |     |       |     |     |     |
|     |     |     |       |     |     |     |
|     |     |     |       |     |     |     |
|     |     |     |       |     |     |     |
|     |     |     |       |     |     |     |
|     |     |     |       |     |     |     |
|     |     |     |       |     |     |     |

# 👉 MONTHLY CHECKLIST

| SHOPPING LIST | KIDS LIST |
|---|---|

★ _____

★ _____

★ _____

★ _____

★ _____

★ _____

★ _____

★ _____

★ _____

★ _____

★ _____

★ _____

★ _____

★ _____

★ _____

★ _____

★ _____

★ _____

DINNER DATES

PLAY DATES

# ☛ KEEP TRACK

## QUOTE OF THE MONTH

## BILLS TO PAY

| | |
|---|---|
| | |
| | |
| | |
| | |
| | |
| | |
| | |
| | |
| | |

## I'M GRATEFUL FOR

## NOTES

# WEEKLY MEETING

MONDAY

FRIDAY

TUESDAY

SATURDAY

WEDNESDAY

SUNDAY

THURSDAY

NOTES

# TO DO

❖
❖
❖
❖
❖
❖
❖
❖
❖

## DINNER MEETINGS

| MON | TUE | WED | THURS |
|-----|-----|-----|-------|
|     |     |     |       |

| FRI | SAT | SUN | |
|-----|-----|-----|---|
|     |     |     | |

## REMINDERS

# MONTHLY PLANNER

| Mon | Tue | Wed | Thurs | Fri | Sat | Sun |
|-----|-----|-----|-------|-----|-----|-----|
|     |     |     |       |     |     |     |
|     |     |     |       |     |     |     |
|     |     |     |       |     |     |     |
|     |     |     |       |     |     |     |
|     |     |     |       |     |     |     |
|     |     |     |       |     |     |     |
|     |     |     |       |     |     |     |
|     |     |     |       |     |     |     |

# 👉 MONTHLY CHECKLIST

| SHOPPING LIST | KIDS LIST |
|---|---|

★ _____

★ _____

★ _____

★ _____

★ _____

★ _____

★ _____

★ _____

★ _____

★ _____

★ _____

★ _____

★ _____

★ _____

★ _____

★ _____

★ _____

★ _____

| DINNER DATES | PLAY DATES |
|---|---|

# 👉 KEEP TRACK

## QUOTE OF THE MONTH

## BILLS TO PAY

|  |  |
|---|---|
|  |  |
|  |  |
|  |  |
|  |  |
|  |  |
|  |  |
|  |  |
|  |  |
|  |  |
|  |  |
|  |  |

## I'M GRATEFUL FOR

## NOTES

# WEEKLY MEETING

MONDAY

FRIDAY

TUESDAY

SATURDAY

WEDNESDAY

SUNDAY

THURSDAY

NOTES

# TO DO

✤      ✤      ✤      ✤

✤      ✤      ✤      ✤

✤      ✤      ✤      ✤

✤      ✤      ✤      ✤

✤      ✤      ✤      ✤

✤      ✤      ✤      ✤

✤      ✤      ✤      ✤

✤      ✤      ✤      ✤

✤      ✤      ✤      ✤

## DINNER MEETINGS

| MON | TUE | WED | THURS |
|-----|-----|-----|-------|
|     |     |     |       |
| FRI | SAT | SUN |       |
|     |     |     |       |

# REMINDERS

# WEEKLY MEETING

| MONDAY | FRIDAY |
|--------|--------|

| TUESDAY | SATURDAY |
|---------|----------|

| WEDNESDAY | SUNDAY |
|-----------|--------|

| THURSDAY | NOTES |
|----------|-------|

# ☞ MONTHLY PLANNER

| Mon | Tue | Wed | Thurs | Fri | Sat | Sun |
|-----|-----|-----|-------|-----|-----|-----|
|     |     |     |       |     |     |     |
|     |     |     |       |     |     |     |
|     |     |     |       |     |     |     |
|     |     |     |       |     |     |     |
|     |     |     |       |     |     |     |
|     |     |     |       |     |     |     |
|     |     |     |       |     |     |     |
|     |     |     |       |     |     |     |

# MONTHLY CHECKLIST

| SHOPPING LIST | KIDS LIST |
|---|---|

★ _____
★ _____
★ _____
★ _____
★ _____
★ _____
★ _____
★ _____
★ _____

★ _____
★ _____
★ _____
★ _____
★ _____
★ _____
★ _____
★ _____
★ _____

| DINNER DATES | PLAY DATES |
|---|---|

👉 # KEEP TRACK

## QUOTE OF THE MONTH

## BILLS TO PAY

## I'M GRATEFUL FOR

## NOTES

# WEEKLY MEETING

| MONDAY | FRIDAY |
|--------|--------|

| TUESDAY | SATURDAY |
|---------|----------|

| WEDNESDAY | SUNDAY |
|-----------|--------|

| THURSDAY | NOTES |
|----------|-------|

# TO DO

❖ | ❖ | ❖ | ❖
❖ | ❖ | ❖ | ❖
❖ | ❖ | ❖ | ❖
❖ | ❖ | ❖ | ❖
❖ | ❖ | ❖ | ❖
❖ | ❖ | ❖ | ❖
❖ | ❖ | ❖ | ❖
❖ | ❖ | ❖ | ❖
❖ | ❖ | ❖ | ❖

## DINNER MEETINGS

| MON | TUE | WED | THURS |
|-----|-----|-----|-------|
| FRI | SAT | SUN | |

## REMINDERS

# ☛ MONTHLY PLANNER

| Mon | Tue | Wed | Thurs | Fri | Sat | Sun |
|-----|-----|-----|-------|-----|-----|-----|
|     |     |     |       |     |     |     |
|     |     |     |       |     |     |     |
|     |     |     |       |     |     |     |
|     |     |     |       |     |     |     |
|     |     |     |       |     |     |     |
|     |     |     |       |     |     |     |
|     |     |     |       |     |     |     |
|     |     |     |       |     |     |     |

# 👉 MONTHLY CHECKLIST

| SHOPPING LIST |
|---|

★ _____
★ _____
★ _____
★ _____
★ _____
★ _____
★ _____
★ _____
★ _____

| KIDS LIST |
|---|

★ _____
★ _____
★ _____
★ _____
★ _____
★ _____
★ _____
★ _____
★ _____

DINNER DATES

PLAY DATES

# 👉 KEEP TRACK

## QUOTE OF THE MONTH

## BILLS TO PAY

|  |  |
|---|---|
|  |  |
|  |  |
|  |  |
|  |  |
|  |  |
|  |  |
|  |  |
|  |  |
|  |  |
|  |  |

## I'M GRATEFUL FOR

## NOTES

# WEEKLY MEETING

| | |
|---|---|
| MONDAY | FRIDAY |
| TUESDAY | SATURDAY |
| WEDNESDAY | SUNDAY |
| THURSDAY | NOTES |

# TO DO

| ❖ | ❖ | ❖ | ❖ |
| ❖ | ❖ | ❖ | ❖ |
| ❖ | ❖ | ❖ | ❖ |
| ❖ | ❖ | ❖ | ❖ |
| ❖ | ❖ | ❖ | ❖ |
| ❖ | ❖ | ❖ | ❖ |
| ❖ | ❖ | ❖ | ❖ |
| ❖ | ❖ | ❖ | ❖ |
| ❖ | ❖ | ❖ | ❖ |

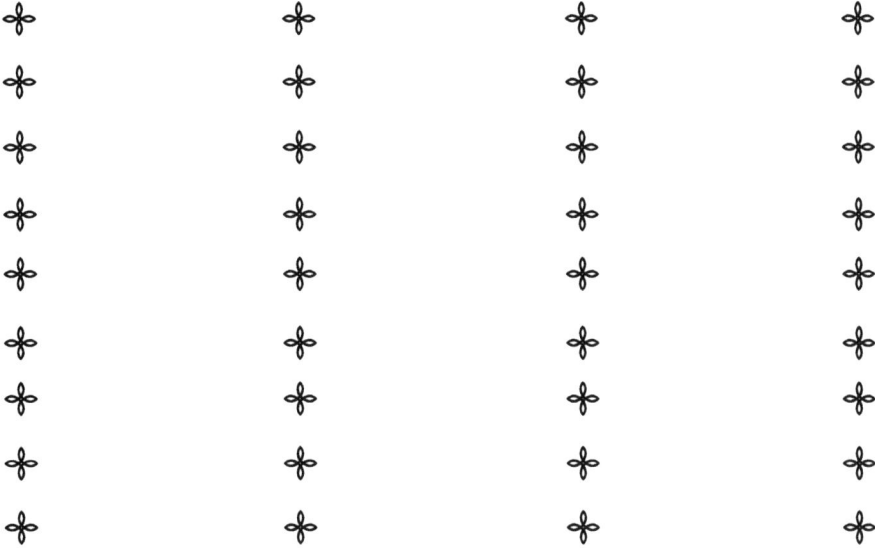

# DINNER MEETINGS

| MON | TUE | WED | THURS |
| FRI | SAT | SUN | |

# REMINDERS

# ☛ MONTHLY CHECKLIST

| SHOPPING LIST | KIDS LIST |
|---|---|

★ _____

★ _____

★ _____

★ _____

★ _____

★ _____

★ _____

★ _____

★ _____

★ _____

★ _____

★ _____

★ _____

★ _____

★ _____

★ _____

★ _____

★ _____

| DINNER DATES | PLAY DATES |
|---|---|

👉 KEEP TRACK

QUOTE OF THE MONTH

BILLS TO PAY

I'M GRATEFUL FOR

NOTES

# WEEKLY MEETING

MONDAY

FRIDAY

TUESDAY

SATURDAY

WEDNESDAY

SUNDAY

THURSDAY

NOTES

# TO DO

| | | | |
|---|---|---|---|
| ❖ | ❖ | ❖ | ❖ |
| ❖ | ❖ | ❖ | ❖ |
| ❖ | ❖ | ❖ | ❖ |
| ❖ | ❖ | ❖ | ❖ |
| ❖ | ❖ | ❖ | ❖ |
| ❖ | ❖ | ❖ | ❖ |
| ❖ | ❖ | ❖ | ❖ |
| ❖ | ❖ | ❖ | ❖ |
| ❖ | ❖ | ❖ | ❖ |

# DINNER MEETINGS

| MON | TUE | WED | THURS |
|---|---|---|---|
| | | | |

| FRI | SAT | SUN | |
|---|---|---|---|
| | | | |

# REMINDERS

# ☞ MONTHLY PLANNER

| Mon | Tue | Wed | Thurs | Fri | Sat | Sun |
|-----|-----|-----|-------|-----|-----|-----|
|     |     |     |       |     |     |     |
|     |     |     |       |     |     |     |
|     |     |     |       |     |     |     |
|     |     |     |       |     |     |     |
|     |     |     |       |     |     |     |
|     |     |     |       |     |     |     |
|     |     |     |       |     |     |     |

# 👉 MONTHLY CHECKLIST

| SHOPPING LIST | KIDS LIST |
|---|---|

★ _____
★ _____
★ _____
★ _____
★ _____
★ _____
★ _____
★ _____
★ _____

★ _____
★ _____
★ _____
★ _____
★ _____
★ _____
★ _____
★ _____
★ _____

| DINNER DATES | PLAY DATES |
|---|---|

# WEEKLY MEETING

MONDAY

FRIDAY

TUESDAY

SATURDAY

WEDNESDAY

SUNDAY

THURSDAY

NOTES

# TO DO

❖          ❖          ❖          ❖

❖          ❖          ❖          ❖

❖          ❖          ❖          ❖

❖          ❖          ❖          ❖

❖          ❖          ❖          ❖

❖          ❖          ❖          ❖

❖          ❖          ❖          ❖

❖          ❖          ❖          ❖

❖          ❖          ❖          ❖

# DINNER MEETINGS

| MON | TUE | WED | THURS |
|-----|-----|-----|-------|
|     |     |     |       |

| FRI | SAT | SUN |   |
|-----|-----|-----|---|
|     |     |     |   |

# REMINDERS

# WEEKLY MEETING

MONDAY

FRIDAY

TUESDAY

SATURDAY

WEDNESDAY

SUNDAY

THURSDAY

NOTES

# ☞ MONTHLY PLANNER

| Mon | Tue | Wed | Thurs | Fri | Sat | Sun |
|-----|-----|-----|-------|-----|-----|-----|
|     |     |     |       |     |     |     |
|     |     |     |       |     |     |     |
|     |     |     |       |     |     |     |
|     |     |     |       |     |     |     |
|     |     |     |       |     |     |     |
|     |     |     |       |     |     |     |
|     |     |     |       |     |     |     |
|     |     |     |       |     |     |     |

# MONTHLY CHECKLIST

| SHOPPING LIST | KIDS LIST |
|---|---|

★ _____

★ _____

★ _____

★ _____

★ _____

★ _____

★ _____

★ _____

★ _____

★ _____

★ _____

★ _____

★ _____

★ _____

★ _____

★ _____

★ _____

★ _____

| DINNER DATES | PLAY DATES |
|---|---|

# 👉 KEEP TRACK

## QUOTE OF THE MONTH

## BILLS TO PAY

|  |  |
|---|---|
|  |  |
|  |  |
|  |  |
|  |  |
|  |  |
|  |  |
|  |  |
|  |  |
|  |  |
|  |  |

## I'M GRATEFUL FOR

## NOTES

# WEEKLY MEETING

MONDAY

FRIDAY

TUESDAY

SATURDAY

WEDNESDAY

SUNDAY

THURSDAY

NOTES

# TO DO

❖ ❖ ❖ ❖
❖ ❖ ❖ ❖
❖ ❖ ❖ ❖
❖ ❖ ❖ ❖
❖ ❖ ❖ ❖
❖ ❖ ❖ ❖
❖ ❖ ❖ ❖
❖ ❖ ❖ ❖
❖ ❖ ❖ ❖

## DINNER MEETINGS

| MON | TUE | WED | THURS |
|-----|-----|-----|-------|
|     |     |     |       |

| FRI | SAT | SUN |  |
|-----|-----|-----|--|
|     |     |     |  |

## REMINDERS

# ☚ MONTHLY PLANNER

| Mon | Tue | Wed | Thurs | Fri | Sat | Sun |
|-----|-----|-----|-------|-----|-----|-----|
|     |     |     |       |     |     |     |
|     |     |     |       |     |     |     |
|     |     |     |       |     |     |     |
|     |     |     |       |     |     |     |
|     |     |     |       |     |     |     |
|     |     |     |       |     |     |     |
|     |     |     |       |     |     |     |

# MONTHLY CHECKLIST

| SHOPPING LIST | KIDS LIST |
|---|---|

★ _____
★ _____
★ _____
★ _____
★ _____
★ _____
★ _____
★ _____
★ _____

★ _____
★ _____
★ _____
★ _____
★ _____
★ _____
★ _____
★ _____
★ _____

| DINNER DATES | PLAY DATES |
|---|---|

# 👉 KEEP TRACK

## QUOTE OF THE MONTH

## BILLS TO PAY

| | |
|---|---|
| | |
| | |
| | |
| | |
| | |
| | |
| | |
| | |
| | |

## I'M GRATEFUL FOR

## NOTES

# WEEKLY MEETING

MONDAY

FRIDAY

TUESDAY

SATURDAY

WEDNESDAY

SUNDAY

THURSDAY

NOTES

# TO DO

❖     ❖     ❖     ❖

❖     ❖     ❖     ❖

❖     ❖     ❖     ❖

❖     ❖     ❖     ❖

❖     ❖     ❖     ❖

❖     ❖     ❖     ❖

❖     ❖     ❖     ❖

❖     ❖     ❖     ❖

❖     ❖     ❖     ❖

# DINNER MEETINGS

| MON | TUE | WED | THURS |
|-----|-----|-----|-------|
|     |     |     |       |

| FRI | SAT | SUN |  |
|-----|-----|-----|--|
|     |     |     |  |

# REMINDERS

# ☛ MONTHLY PLANNER

| Mon | Tue | Wed | Thurs | Fri | Sat | Sun |
|---|---|---|---|---|---|---|
|  |  |  |  |  |  |  |
|  |  |  |  |  |  |  |
|  |  |  |  |  |  |  |
|  |  |  |  |  |  |  |
|  |  |  |  |  |  |  |
|  |  |  |  |  |  |  |
|  |  |  |  |  |  |  |
|  |  |  |  |  |  |  |

# ☛ MONTHLY CHECKLIST

| SHOPPING LIST | KIDS LIST |
|---|---|

★ _____

★ _____

★ _____

★ _____

★ _____

★ _____

★ _____

★ _____

★ _____

★ _____

★ _____

★ _____

★ _____

★ _____

★ _____

★ _____

★ _____

★ _____

| DINNER DATES | PLAY DATES |
|---|---|

# 👉 KEEP TRACK

## QUOTE OF THE MONTH

## BILLS TO PAY

## I'M GRATEFUL FOR

## NOTES

# TO DO

✦ ✦ ✦ ✦

✦ ✦ ✦ ✦

✦ ✦ ✦ ✦

✦ ✦ ✦ ✦

✦ ✦ ✦ ✦

✦ ✦ ✦ ✦

✦ ✦ ✦ ✦

✦ ✦ ✦ ✦

✦ ✦ ✦ ✦

## DINNER MEETINGS

| MON | TUE | WED | THURS |
|-----|-----|-----|-------|
|     |     |     |       |

| FRI | SAT | SUN | |
|-----|-----|-----|--|
|     |     |     |  |

## REMINDERS

# WEEKLY MEETING

| | |
|---|---|
| MONDAY | FRIDAY |
| TUESDAY | SATURDAY |
| WEDNESDAY | SUNDAY |
| THURSDAY | NOTES |

# 👉 MONTHLY PLANNER

| Mon | Tue | Wed | Thurs | Fri | Sat | Sun |
|-----|-----|-----|-------|-----|-----|-----|
|     |     |     |       |     |     |     |
|     |     |     |       |     |     |     |
|     |     |     |       |     |     |     |
|     |     |     |       |     |     |     |
|     |     |     |       |     |     |     |
|     |     |     |       |     |     |     |
|     |     |     |       |     |     |     |
|     |     |     |       |     |     |     |

# ☛ MONTHLY CHECKLIST

| SHOPPING LIST | KIDS LIST |
|---|---|

★ _____
★ _____
★ _____
★ _____
★ _____
★ _____
★ _____
★ _____
★ _____

★ _____
★ _____
★ _____
★ _____
★ _____
★ _____
★ _____
★ _____
★ _____

| DINNER DATES | PLAY DATES |
|---|---|

# 👉 KEEP TRACK

## QUOTE OF THE MONTH

## BILLS TO PAY

| | |
|---|---|
| | |
| | |
| | |
| | |
| | |
| | |
| | |
| | |
| | |
| | |

## I'M GRATEFUL FOR

## NOTES

Lightning Source UK Ltd.
Milton Keynes UK
UKHW031820230123
415835UK00007B/571

9 781683 778486